Sticker Dolly Dressing
Fashion Designer
Winter Collection

Designed and illustrated by Stella Baggott

Additional illustrations by Antonia Miller

Written by Fiona Watt

Contents

How to use this book

These pages will give you some hints and tips about using the stickers to create different outfits for dressing the dolls and how to decorate this book.

The stickers

If you look at the sticker pages you will see that some of the stickers are blank, some have patterns on them and some are fully coloured.

Colour in or draw patterns on the plain stickers.

Colour in the shapes on the stickers.

Use the coloured stickers just as they are.

Warning!
The sticker paper is quite smooth, so if you are using felt-tip pens, leave the sticker for a little while before you peel it off. This will give the ink time to dry.

Ideas to try

Below are examples of patterns you could draw on the plain stickers. There are also more ideas for them later in the book.

Samples of materials like these are known as 'swatches'.

Choosing an outfit

All the stickers fit on all the dolls in the book. They are arranged to match different themes, but you can mix and match them as much as you like. There are extra stickers too, to give you lots of choice for different outfits.

Top Tip
It's a good idea to colour in the stickers while they are still on the sticker pages, just in case you go over the edge of the shapes.

Complete an outfit with accessories, such as a hat.

You could add stitching with a thin pen.

Choose a bag that goes with the outfit.

Try colouring in a pale colour and add darker details on top.

Mood boards

Fashion designers make 'mood boards' to show where they got their ideas for colours, materials and the style of their clothes.

Fill the empty space with stickers to make a mood board.

Ideas for colours to use on the stickers

You'll find pictures and photos on some of the stickers. Use these to decorate the pages, once you have designed the outfits.

Winter coats

Use the stickers to create warm, winter outfits for the dolls in shades of red, green and blue. Then, add accessories to match.

Fill the space above with swatches and photographs from the sticker pages.

Ideas for colours to use

Nordic knits

Designers sometimes decorate their winter fashions with patterns inspired by traditional Scandinavian knitting.

Colour in these winter hats.

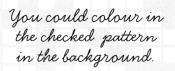

You could colour in the checked pattern in the background.

Party dresses

Mix or match the stickers to create party outfits for the dolls. Combine yellow, red, pink and black with shoes to match.

Ski wear

A Winter Collection wouldn't be complete without some cosy ski wear. Dress the dolls in outfits suitable for a day on the slopes or a walk in the snow.

Design your own swatches
by colouring in the
patterns above.

Evening gown

Decorate this gown with stickers to give it some sparkle. You could make a pattern with the stickers and then add details of your own.

Press the stickers of the swatches onto the circles above.

Put the glove stickers on the dolls
before adding the coats.

Winter berries

Nordic knits pages 6-7

Use shades of red, blue and purple to add rows of patterns to the plain stickers.

Party dresses pages 8-9

You could decorate the stickers
with hearts, spots and flowers.

Stickers for the
background

Put the trousers on the dolls before
you add the jackets and boots.

Evening gown   page 12

Use the stickers to design a sparkling evening dress for the doll on page 12.

Cosy cape   page 13

Put the trousers on the doll before adding the boots.

Christmas jumpers
pages 16-17

Use your imagination to design
a picture or a pattern for a
Christmas jumper.

*Stickers for the
background or use one
as a motif on a jumper.*

For coordinated clothes, use the colours on the dots below to decorate the stickers.

A cape

Pyjama party

pages 20-21

Put the pyjamas on the dolls
before adding the slippers.

Select stickers for the dolls on pages 22-23. You could use the spare ones on other pages in the book.

Cosy cape

Design an outfit for a walk on a crisp winter's day. Complete the look with cosy accessories.

You could colour in the design in the background.

Masked ball

Design outfits for the dolls to wear to a masked ball. You could decorate the dresses with patterns or lace, inspired by snowflakes.

Colour the masks
in icy shades.

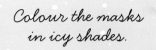

You could draw
layers of lace on
this dress.

Christmas jumpers

What would you choose to wear on the front of a festive jumper - a snowman, Santa or a red-nosed reindeer? Give each doll a jumper, then shoes or boots, and a hat to match.

You could colour
in decorations in
the background.

Ice skating

Design the outfits for a warm-up session before an ice dance competition. Give each doll a pair of skates which coordinate with her clothes.

Fill in the skates using these colours.

Pyjama party

Imagine the dolls are going to a pyjama party. Use soft, pastel shades to decorate their sleepwear and slippers.

Use the swatch
stickers and
photographs to
decorate this page.

Keeping warm

Complete the outfits with different accessories by adding a hat or ear muffs and a scarf to each doll.

Design your own sketchbook

You could start a sketchbook of your own fashion ideas. Trace over or copy the template of the doll, then use any leftover stickers to create some new outfits. Instead of using stickers to decorate your doll you could draw the clothes instead.

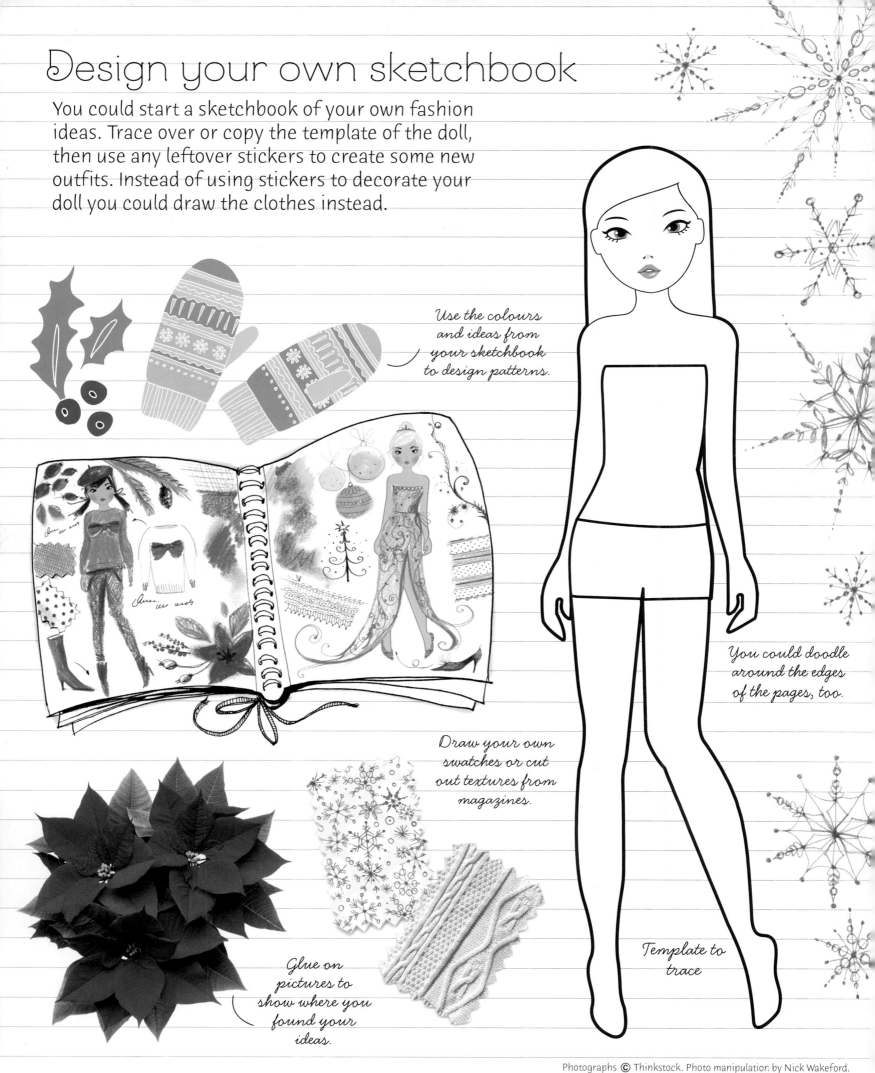

Use the colours and ideas from your sketchbook to design patterns.

You could doodle around the edges of the pages, too.

Draw your own swatches or cut out textures from magazines.

Glue on pictures to show where you found your ideas.

Template to trace

Photographs © Thinkstock. Photo manipulation by Nick Wakeford.
First published in 2014 by Usborne Publishing Ltd., Usborne House , 83-85 Saffron Hill, London, EC1N 8RT, England. www.usborne.com Copyright © 2014 Usborne Publishing Ltd